VIETNAM

THE MEMOIR
OF A
SANDLOT SOLDIER

W. THOMAS BURNS

VIETNAM

THE MEMOIR
OF A
SANDLOT SOLDIER

VIETNAM

THE MEMOIR
OF A
SANDLOT SOLDIER

W. THOMAS BURNS

Vietnam The Memoir of a Sandlot Soldier

Copyright © 2022 William Thomas Burns

Printed in the United States of America
ISBN 978-1-956543-06-3 (softcover)
ISBN 978-1-956543-11-7 (hardcover)

Book design by CSinclaire Write-Design
Cover design by Klevur

WRITEWAY
PUBLISHING

This book is dedicated to all

who have served our country in any capacity

throughout the history of our nation

and

to the many Gold Star Families

whose sons and daughters have given their lives

for the freedoms that

all of us as Americans enjoy.

Contents

IN APPRECIATION IX

ACKNOWLEDGMENTS XI

GROWING UP IN THE GOOD OLD USA 1

TRAINING DAYS 4

OUR ARRIVAL IN VIETNAM 7

THE ENEMY—THEY LOOKED JUST LIKE US 10

THE YOUNG CORPORAL TAKES THE POINT 17

COMBAT OPERATIONS IN THE MOUNTAINS OF VIETNAM 19

THE LEGEND OF L/CPL TAMILIO TAMBURINI 21

HILL 606, JULY 1968 24

THE HEROISM OF THE YOUNG NAVY CORPSMAN 30

STAFF SERGEANT D. J. HINSON TAKES OVER 33

THE RECON MISSION ON THE BEN HAI RIVER 41

OPERATION PURPLE MARTIN 46

THE WAR WAS OVER FOR THE WOUNDED 48

THE M-16 RIFLE 50

A MARINE'S MARINE 51

W. THOMAS BURNS 66

ABOUT THE AUTHOR 81

In Appreciation

If it were not for the long hours on the computer
by my wife, Stella—"Star"—
this book would be nothing more than
a bunch of old photographs and
a pile of misspelled and scribbled notes
stuffed away in a dark and musty corner of the attic.

Thank you, my darling, for a life I never dreamed I'd live.

Acknowledgments

My thanks to former United States Marine, Staff Sergeant Dennis G. Pregent, a Vietnam Veteran. Dennis is an accomplished author in his own right. I would highly suggest picking up a copy of his book *The Boys of St. Joe's '65 in the Vietnam War*, an outstanding insight into the lives and families of the generation of young patriots who grew up in small town America, then found themselves fighting for their lives in Vietnam. He follows the lives of his boyhood friends after the war from dealing with their combat injuries to their memories of the horrors of that war.

When I was lost and had no idea where to turn, Dennis recommended Jane Hobson Snyder, an editor that he has been working with for several years. Jane is from Raleigh, NC, and has no equal with regard to her editorial expertise.

When the time came to find a publishing company, Jane highly recommended Lee Heinrich at WriteWay Publishing of Raleigh, NC. At that time, this inexperienced writer began the final stage of his journey toward the publication of this book. I contacted Lee and thus began one of the greatest experiences of my life. For it was then that Lee, who surrounds herself with her team of professionals at WriteWay Publishing that includes graphic designer and lead book formatter Charlotte Sinclaire, a cover design team, and Kaili Wardlaw who coordinated the team that was responsible for the author's photograph found within my website and book cover, took me through the stages of my publishing journey.

It has been a pleasure working with Lee for she has an uncommon style and grace about her and I might add a sense of humor that can brighten up even the dreariest of days. Thank you, Lee, for making my dream come true. I shall forever be grateful.

— *W. Thomas Burns*

VIETNAM

THE MEMOIR
OF A
SANDLOT SOLDIER

Growing Up in the Good Old USA

The story that I am about to tell has to do with the lives and times of the generation of Americans who grew up in the 1950s and the 1960s. Some would say those were the best of times to be a kid in the good old USA.

Our generation grew up on sandlots across America. It was there that we learned the lessons of teamwork, self-determination, and what it took to win. The sandlots were the ideal training grounds for those of us who aspired to be our country's next generation of United States Marines.

Our school days were spent learning the important subjects of reading, writing, and arithmetic. Our favorite time of the day was, of course, recess. Stickball, tag, and, during the winter months, snowball fights and king of the mountain were always on the agenda. The foundations of many friendships were formed on those playgrounds and ball fields and in the caddy shacks of the local golf courses.

Can anyone imagine that a whole generation of young American boys fell in love with the most beautiful and talented girl in the world? The images of that young girl were brought to us some sixty years ago via television by none other than the magical creativity of Walt Disney. (Thank you, Annette, from all of us. Thanks for the memories.)

Both of my parents were veterans of World War II, as were the fathers of most of my friends. We were brought up to believe in God, country, and the American way. Our patriotism was reinforced by the many Hollywood depictions of some of our nation's heroes, past and present. Heroes that included Daniel Boone, Davy Crockett, Sgt. Alvin York, Audie Murphy, and The Fighting Sullivan Brothers. Many gave some, some gave all. Little did we know at that time we were to be our country's next generation of warriors, "The Sandlot Soldiers."

Our high school years were filled with sandlot sports, hanging out at the corner soda fountain, and part-time jobs. Our main interests during those years were primarily centered around girls, the game of golf, and old Fords and Chevys. I can't say that we spent much time hitting the books, but those years were fun—high school dances, Levi jeans, penny loafers, and hanging out with friends at Richie's soda fountain.

College was certainly not for everyone, but I will say that those who did fill the halls of our great universities most likely fared better than those who didn't.

Then in the mid-1960s came the rumors of war. A conflict in which our country had become involved. A war that was being fought by our generation of young American patriots. This was the first war ever to be broadcast into the living room of every American family on the six o'clock news: "Good evening, this is Walter Cronkite reporting."

Over the next few years, that conflict escalated dramatically and the number of casualties among our young American warriors grew to unimaginable numbers.

That war was being fought in a land unknown to most Americans, a region once called French Indochina and currently known as the Republic of Vietnam.

Training Days

M y military training began in late November 1967, just prior to the Tet Offensive of 1968. During the flight to a recruit training base at Parris Island, South Carolina, I remember thinking how grateful our drill instructors would be when we arrived. After all, we had made the decision to leave our comfortable lives and join the war effort in whatever capacity our country saw fit. We had come from the north and the south, the east and the west, and from the heartland of our nation to follow in the footsteps of those who came before us. Our common goal was to become a United States Marine.

Needless to say, our greeting by the drill instructors did not go exactly the way I had anticipated. There was a lot of yelling and screaming going on. Then came the yellow footprints, military-style haircuts, and new utility uniforms. I can't say they were custom-fit, but they did the job. No talking, eyes forward, yes sir, no sir, then more yelling and screaming. It was approximately two a.m. when we finally got to sleep, and wouldn't you know, at five a.m. the yelling and screaming started again. (On what planet did they find these nutcases? Grown men in Smokey-the-Bear hats and custom-tailored uniforms running around and screaming all the time.)

It was about that time we realized we were on an isolated island with what appeared to be hundreds of escapees from a lunatic asylum (drill instructors) making nuisances of themselves and obviously in need of some serious medication. It was then that we decided we would just have to put up with their insanity for the next eight weeks and then we would be done with them.

As the weeks wore on and our training progressed, we grew to respect those drill instructors for they were some of America's finest, the best of the best; they had proven themselves with their leadership skills and, most importantly, with their valor on the fields of battle. Upon graduation from recruit training, the top 10 percent of our platoon were rewarded with promotions to Private First Class, indeed, a great honor for them.

The second phase of our training took place at an infantry training facility in North Carolina. There was a lot less yelling and scream-ing going on there, and we were grateful for that. During our time at Camp Lejeune, we were taught infantry tactics and were trained in the use of many types of weapons that included M-1 rifles, M-23 grenades, and M-60 machine guns. Our evolution from civilians to United States military personnel was progressing. We could see the changes in ourselves and in our fellow trainees.

After the completion of the second phase of our training, another 10 percent of us were promoted to PFC. It was an honor to be recognized by our staff and officers. We had no intention of letting them down.

When we finished our four weeks of advanced infantry training, we flew home on military leave. To be perfectly honest, I don't remember anything about those days at home. When my leave was up, I boarded an American Airlines jet just outside of Hartford, Connecticut, flew cross-country, and landed at a large military base in California for four more weeks of training.

At the end of this third phase of training at Camp Pendleton, we were off to Southeast Asia. One thing I do remember about that flight was that the closer we got to our destination, the quieter the sandlot soldiers became.

Our Arrival
in Vietnam

I was born on the fourth of May in 1949 and arrived in Vietnam on the fourth of May in 1968 along with hundreds of other young Marines. Our goal was to fight for what we believed in.

Upon our arrival in Vietnam, we were issued our combat gear that included an M-16 rifle, M-23 grenades, extra belts of machine gun ammunition, twenty magazines of M-16 ammunition, and combat boots.

And there we stood, the sandlot soldiers, all dressed in camouflage utilities and combat gear. At that time, we were told by the officer in charge that we were the finest fighting military force in the world. Really? What a miraculous transformation we had made from bell bottoms, rock and roll, and high school football games after a grand total of four months of hurry-up combat training.

But I will say this, we did have a lot going for us. We believed in ourselves. We were proud to be our nation's newest combat Marines, and we had no intention of being anything other than the best Marines that we could possibly be, and that was that.

The rumor was that we were to be replacements for a Marine combat unit, the 2nd Battalion, 4th Marine Regiment, 3rd Marine Division, that had fought so valiantly only days before against a six- to eight-thousand-man division of North Vietnamese Army soldiers.

I didn't know until forty years later, due to the miracle of the internet, that the Marine casualty count from the battle of Dai Do, also known as the Battle of Dong Ha, was 81 U.S. Marine personnel killed in action and 234 wounded in action. The number of enemy soldiers killed during that battle was estimated to have been 2,945. May our country never forget those young Marines for the sacrifices they made during that three-day battle that was fought from April 30 through May 2, 1968.

On May 6, 1968, we were transported by helicopter to Camp Big John, a hastily assembled staging area with the sole purpose of distributing ammunition and re-supplies to the Marines who had fought the Battle of Dai Do against the 320th North Vietnamese Army Division. Camp Big John was named in honor of Sgt. Major John Marion Malnar, a legendary Marine who was killed in action on May 2, 1968 during that battle.

The camp was located several miles south of the DMZ. On that day, just before sunset, our unit came under attack by several enemy soldiers firing AK-47 rifles. They had popped up out of the brush approximately 75-80 yards from our perimeter. They were immediately cut down by one of our machine gunners. As we watched our first encounter with the enemy, I can remember having no emotions, no feelings whatsoever, with regard to the deaths of those NVA soldiers. They were the enemy. End of day one in Vietnam.

We would soon find out that it wasn't always going to be that easy. The next day we were assigned to squads, platoons, and companies.

We were designated as First Squad, 3rd Platoon, Golf Company. Golf Company—how ironic!

That afternoon we met our first squad leader, Sgt. Milano. He was a twenty-something-year-old Italian American farm boy from the Midwest, a highly trained reconnaissance Marine who was on his second tour of duty in Vietnam. He could have been a poster Marine, quiet, farm strong, and self-confident. We learned a lot from him over the next several months, and we considered ourselves very fortunate to have him as our squad leader.

The Enemy—They Looked Just Like Us

A few days later, our platoon of approximately thirty men was sent out on patrol. The sky was completely devoid of any cloud cover. It was hot and humid. The area that we were patrolling consisted of rice paddies, waist high grass, and some trees growing along the rice paddy dikes. At approximately one hour into our patrol, we came upon two NVA soldiers hiding in the brush. They were completely unaware of our presence. Moments later, they were both dead. Some of the old timers went through their backpacks and the pockets of their uniforms, finding, among other things, photographs of these now deceased NVA soldiers in civilian clothes with their young Vietnamese girlfriends. They looked just like us.

Later that week, approximately twenty of us went out on a night roving ambush. We made our way to four or five checkpoints during the course of the night and returned back to base the next morning without incident. Within a few hours of our return, we learned that our starlight scope had gone missing while on that patrol. That was unfortunate, but as far as we were concerned, we had returned safely having taken no casualties, so in our minds, it was a successful mission.

We had all been issued a set of two military dog tags, one of which we wore on a chain around our neck, the other we wove into the laces of one of our combat boots. The dog tags were made of aluminum. Our name, serial number, branch of service, religious affiliation, and blood type was pressed into each of them.

On May 12, 1968, just eight days into our tour, we went out on a company-size search-and-destroy operation with approximately ninety men. That operation was in the same general area that we had been working for the past week. We had only been out for a few hours when we made contact with the enemy.

An NVA soldier, who was hiding in a spider trap, shot and killed the squad leader of another squad. After that enemy soldier was eliminated, we pushed on and became involved in a large-scale firefight. As we moved forward, we encountered a number of dead enemy soldiers lying in the brush. At that time, Sgt. Milano told me to drop back fifty or sixty yards and set up as the rear security to ensure that our unit was not approached from the rear by the enemy.

As I moved from my position into the open, I came under enemy fire. It was just like in the movies. AK-47 rounds were dancing in the dirt around me. Within a few minutes, I had reached my assigned position with the intention of not allowing the enemy to attack my unit from the rear. The firefight was still raging behind me, and small-arms rounds were flying everywhere. I then observed what first appeared to be twelve Vietnamese rice paddy workers wearing only shorts and walking single file on the rice paddy dike to the left of where the firefight was taking place. I did not have a radio, so I yelled to Sgt. Milano and reported the situation.

The firefight was still in full force when the farm boy from the Midwest yelled back and told me to just keep an eye on them. As the group of twelve continued along the dike, which also ran parallel to my position, I made the observation that the man in the lead was probably in his mid-forties and very fit, as were all of the younger men that followed him. They were barefoot. The closer they got to my position, the more I suspected that they were, in all probability, NVA soldiers who had stripped down in order to flee the battlefield.

What to do? I could have eliminated a number of them, but they appeared to be unarmed. I could have ordered them to stop and attempted to take them prisoners, or I could follow orders and continue acting as rear security for my unit, which is what I decided to do. The events of that day have haunted me for more than fifty years.

I have no idea how many enemy soldiers were killed that day, nor do I know how many of them were wounded. As we made our way on foot back to our base camp, we were passed by a military vehicle that was carrying the bodies of several Marines. We later found out that a young Mexican American Marine with whom we had trained was among the dead. We spent that night in our foxholes remembering PFC Paul Alaniz, a friend and fellow Marine, who lost his life during that battle. Four U.S. Marines were killed in action that day. I do not know how many Marines were wounded.

One of the enemy's combat tactics revolved around the use of a small camouflage position called a spider trap. An NVA soldier would dig a three-foot-wide by four-foot-deep hole in the ground, usually just feet off to the side of a trail. They were well camouflaged and literally undetectable until we were right on top of them. The spider traps were responsible for many U.S. casualties during the Vietnam war.

The next day, Sgt. Milano called me to his foxhole and asked me what I thought about walking point for the squad. Of course, I accepted. I liked being in the lead. That way I had some control over my own destiny and the destinies of the sandlot soldiers that followed. As it turned out, Corporal Garvey, a good friend from Louisville, Kentucky, decided that he was also up to the challenge. We walked point together for the next several months until his tour of duty in Vietnam ended. It was good to see him return to "the world" all in one piece, uninjured and unharmed. I was quite sure that he would be successful in whatever path he chose in life. He was a fine Marine and respected by all.

It didn't take long for the black finish on our new combat boots to wear off. The boots were soon worn and turned to the colors of sand and light green, much more suitable for blending in with the terrain.

When we were first issued our combat gear, we did not realize how important our "entrenching tool" (small shovel) would be in our daily quest to stay alive. Some would say that it was as important a piece of equipment as our rifle was. At that point in my combat tour in Vietnam, the days and nights were becoming a blur.

We owned the daylight hours, and the enemy owned the night. Late every afternoon we would stop and set up a night defensive perimeter. That meant digging foxholes and setting up trip flares and claymore mines out in front of our fighting position. As the day turned to night, we always kept a portion of our team on night watch. The number of men on watch would be determined by the likelihood of being attacked by the enemy. The most unacceptable offense a Marine could make was to fall asleep while on night watch. If he were to do so, he would put the lives of his team members in grave danger. Although that did not happen very often, anyone who fell asleep would be subject to severe repercussions.

It is not my intention to write of each and every engagement with the enemy and, to be honest, many of them are just flashing images of which I do not remember specifics.

Cpl. Garvey, Golf 2/4, Louisville, KY. A friend and respected by all. Vietnam, October 1968

Golf 2/4 Marines, Cliff, Holly, Cpl. Garvey, the Author, Combat Base Vandegrift, Vietnam, November 1968

Back in the rear with
Lance Corporal Bob Lapham
A good friend from
Middleton, MA.
Vietnam, 1969

Mail call, Golf 2/4.
Bob, the most popular
Marine in the Company.
Vietnam, February 1969

The Young Corporal
Takes the Point

In late May of 1968, a young corporal just coming off of embassy duty in Canada arrived at our unit as a replacement. He was assigned to be our fire-team leader. A few days later, we went out on a platoon-size patrol, approximately thirty men. Normally I would have walked point that day, but Marine Corporal Michael Hall decided that he wanted to take the lead. We were all impressed. Some among us were apprehensive after hearing that a Marine Recon team had reported that the enemy had been frequenting the area that we were heading into.

We made our way through the rice paddies and the waist-high grass that dominated the landscape. The ever-present humidity was the least of our concerns that morning. Little did we know that the courageous young corporal who had volunteered to take point that morning would not survive the day. I have, over these many years, often thought about that heroic young Marine.

We were only three weeks into our tour of duty in Vietnam and the possibility of our surviving twelve months and twenty days in that environment did not seem likely.

While in the mountains and the jungles of Vietnam, Navy medics called corpsmen took care of our combat casualties. There were usually two corpsmen assigned to each platoon of approximately twenty-five men. We had the ultimate respect for them. They were the real heroes, always making their way, usually under enemy fire, to the wounded Marines on the battlefield with complete disregard for their own safety. One thing that most people don't know is that Navy corpsmen and Army medics, as a group, are the most decorated of all combat veterans. They have saved the lives of many young American soldiers throughout the years.

Combat Operations in the Mountains of Vietnam

On June 20, 1968, our company of approximately one hundred Marines boarded helicopters at Dong Ha Combat Base and was transported to Hill 512. Hill 512 was one of the hills that overlooked the combat base at Khe Sanh. It was our first time in the mountains of Vietnam. Engineers and a construction battalion were destroying the base and the air strip at Khe Sanh so that it could not be used by the enemy in the future. We were there to discourage the NVA from taking advantage of the situation.

It was very hot in Vietnam at that time of the year. The enemy mortared our position several times a day for the entire time that we were there. When we weren't standing perimeter guard or running daily patrols in the area surrounding the hill, we were digging foxholes, filling sandbags, and building bunkers. It really is amazing how much the human body can endure when it comes right down to life-and-death situations. I have no idea how many casualties we took during that month. By that time, I had long given up trying to keep track.

Then on July 20, 1968, the word was passed to saddle up. The rumor mill was running wild. We're going back to the rear! We're going back to the rear. Wrong again. When the choppers picked us up, they flew west, deeper into the mountains where we ran combat operations for the remainder of my tour in Vietnam.

The author and the fine art of bunker building. Dry as a bone and built to withstand just about anything. Vietnam, October 1968

The Legend of L/Cpl Tamilio Tamburini

I don't remember exactly when Tami joined our squad, but I do remember how he arrived. We were on a hill somewhere in the mountains when a resupply chopper landed in a cloud of dust.

L/Cpl Tami T., Toledo, OH. A fearless combat Marine with the heart of a lion.

And from that cloud of dust emerged a somewhat mythical figure. A newcomer, whose name we did not yet know, jumped off that chopper with hands on hips as if to announce his arrival. To say the least, he was quite a sight. A young Sicilian American Marine from Toledo, Ohio, with all the swagger and self-confidence a man could possibly have. And there he stood, a camouflage beret upon his head and a large bowie knife strapped to his leg. It was as if we were on the set of a Hollywood movie. Our savior had arrived! As it turned out, Tami was an outstanding addition to our squad and a great deal of fun to be around.

When we moved into the mountains, the weight of our backpacks and battle gear became a serious issue. I would guess they averaged around sixty to seventy pounds, almost half the body weight of many of our eighteen- and nineteen-year-old Marines. It's one thing to carry that kind of weight in the flatlands and quite another to carry it in the mountains.

Whenever the opportunity presented itself, we would pick up enemy backpacks on the battlefields and use them as our own. They were of a much better quality and design than the haversacks that we had been issued. At one point during our tour in Vietnam, we spent fifty-six consecutive days humping our way through the mountains, oftentimes on our hands and knees. The wear and tear on our bodies has been, to this day, an issue for many.

When we moved from the flatlands into the mountains, spider traps were not as big of an issue, but there were other obstacles that were even more lethal. We had to be constantly aware of the well-camouflaged enemy bunkers, bunker complexes, and underground tunnel systems. It wasn't until many years after the war had ended that we came to understand just exactly how extensive the enemy's underground complexes were.

CH 47 Helicopter. Marines' main form of transportation while in Vietnam.

Hill 606, July 1968

In late July of 1968, a recon team had reported enemy activity on Hill 606. We were told to prepare for a company-size combat operation of approximately one hundred Marines. A short time later, the word was passed for us to saddle up. The helicopters picked us up first thing in the morning. When we reached our destination, we jumped off the choppers about 500 meters to the south of our objective, Hill 606. The terrain was a combination of gentle hills, grassland, and mountains. It was hot and humid.

We reached the base of our objective at approximately two p.m. Since we believed the hilltop was occupied by a large number of entrenched enemy soldiers, the first platoon, approximately thirty men, was ordered to assault the hill. The other two platoons would remain in reserve and be prepared to respond as necessary.

When the first platoon reached the top of the hill, they found it unoccupied. The remainder of the company was soon on the hilltop digging in and preparing to defend our newly acquired position against a possible enemy attack. Not more than twenty minutes had passed when a Marine on watch on the north side of the hill spotted

an enemy patrol of approximately ten NVA soldiers moving casu-
ally across an open area. They were completely unaware that they
were being observed by the Marines. The ideal situation would have
called for us to set up two or three machine guns and open fire on
the unsuspecting enemy patrol and that would have been that. But
that's not how it went.

What actually happened that afternoon was that the lone Marine
took it upon himself, without orders, to fire his M-16 rifle at the
NVA squad that was approximately 400 yards away. That squad of
enemy soldiers ran the final 100 yards through the waist-high grass
and faded away into the jungle. Mistakes of that magnitude on the
battlefield can often be very costly. At that time, the second platoon
was ordered to descend the hill and to engage the enemy. Not long
after they had left the hill, the word was passed that the second
platoon had walked into an ambush and that the point man and
several others were either killed or wounded. After sustaining heavy
casualties, the second platoon broke off contact with the NVA and
returned to the hill.

I would guess that it was approximately four p.m. when the third
platoon was ordered to leave the hill and re-engage with the enemy.
When I took the point that afternoon, I had a very good idea, based on
the direction of the sounds of the second platoon's fire-fight, approximately where the enemy had positioned themselves. I followed the
trail to a point where I felt it was no longer safe to continue in that
direction. I then turned to the right, ascended a small sand-covered
hill and proceeded through an old B-52 bomb crater.

Soon after, we positioned ourselves in a half-circle formation
approximately 40 to 50 yards to the east of where we suspected the
enemy positions were, then all hell broke loose. One of our Marines
put several rounds in the chest of an NVA soldier. The fire-fight

continued, and a heroic Marine from Massachusetts was shot and killed. It was approximately one hour before dark when the third platoon broke contact with the enemy and returned to the hill, taking with us our dead and wounded.

When we reached the top of Hill 606, we were ordered to put on our helmets and flak jackets and start digging in to get as far below the surface of the ground as we possibly could. The Phantoms were on their way.

It wasn't long before the jets arrived. Our fearless brothers in the sky bombarded the enemy's position and quickly vanished into the sunset. We were so close to the impact zone that our entire company was showered with shrapnel, leading to the death of yet another young Golf 2/4 Marine. Five of our Marines were killed in action and an untold number were wounded during that day's firefights with the enemy.

I wish I could say that that was the end of the battle of Hill 606, but it wasn't. The next day the rain began, and soon after, the enemy started showering our position with 122 mm rockets. The rockets were being fired from a mountain top approximately one day's march from our location. We immediately saddled up and began to move out. The rain continued throughout the day. It was late afternoon when we arrived at the base of that mountain. We were told not to dig in but to shelter in place. We were also told that at sunrise, we would assault the enemy's mountain top position. Now wasn't that just Yankee Doodle dandy!

It was widely known that wherever the NVA had rocket positions, they were defended by a large number of infantry solders. Needless to say, none of us got much sleep that night. By that time our numbers had been significantly depleted due to the large number of casualties that we had sustained over the last several days.

It continued to rain throughout the night and into the morning, but the good news was that we were going back to Hill 606. There would be no assault on the enemy's mountain top position that day. We were, to say the least, relieved, and we would more than likely live to fight another day.

Captain Dwyer knew that it would have been nothing less than a suicide mission for a Marine company of approximately ninety men to attempt to assault that mountain without air support, without artillery support, and with no Marines in reserve. Thank God for the rain.

It was late afternoon when we saw the outline of Hill 606 in the distance. Then the word was passed that another Marine company had been flown in and taken over the Hill, thus there was no longer room for us there.

It was getting dark, so we set up for the night on a small grassy knoll within sight of Hill 606. The rumor was that we would be choppered back to the rear in the morning. Thank God for little miracles. We were exhausted, and we all had lost a lot of weight over the last month or so. We were in dire need of some down time.

Then at approximately four a.m., all hell broke loose when a number of enemy satchel charges began exploding inside our perimeter. The enemy sappers were inside our lines. Chaos ensued until the Marines pushed them back and re-secured our position. We took care of the wounded, cleaned up what we could, stayed alert, and prepared for a mass attack by the enemy, an attack that never came.

At sunrise, our leaders took a casualty count. Five more Marines had been killed in action and approximately the same number were wounded during that pre-dawn attack by the enemy. The bottom line is that we had gotten our asses kicked for the whole time we were out on that Godforsaken combat operation.

That's what happens, all too often, when you go into the enemy's own backyard. It's like chasing ghosts until they get you where they want you.

I will leave it up to the reader to assess the facts with regard to this combat operation to establish their own opinions as to why a company of sandlot soldiers was so badly defeated in late July and early August of 1968. I have my own opinions! [Note: When I decided to write about my experiences in Vietnam after all these years, fifty years to be exact, I had no intention of using the word I, but this writer can only bring to the reader that which I had experienced while serving my country during the war in 1968 and 1969.]

It wasn't long after our Hill 606 experience that our squad leader, Sgt. Milano, the farm boy from the Midwest, finished his second tour in Vietnam. We were glad that he had survived and was now on his way back to his family. He would be missed, but not forgotten. Sometime later, I was promoted to corporal and took the lead of the first squad.

Over the next several months, we continued to run company-size operations in the mountains to the west of Quang Tri and inside the DMZ. We would, on occasion, spend a few days at some of the landing zones in northern I Corps, bases like Camp Carol, L Z Vandergrift, and numerous others. During those months, there were encounters with the enemy, but one in particular comes to mind.

Corporal Vern Coy, Golf 2/4. Lincoln, NE. Good friend with a great attitude. Vietnam

The author and Corporal Vern Coy from Lincoln, NE. February of 1969 at L Z Vandergrift, Vietnam

Golf 2/4 Marine. Birthday cake delivered by resupply helicopter.

The Heroism of the Young Navy Corpsman

A few days before a firefight, a young Navy corpsman was assigned to our platoon. He looked like a boy, not yet a man. We had our doubts as to whether he would be capable of performing his duties during the chaos of a firefight. We didn't have to wait long to find out. Soon after his arrival, our platoon of about twenty-five men was moving through a valley in the mountains when we were ambushed by the enemy. One of our Marines was seriously wounded.

A call for "Corpsman Up" rang out. And wouldn't you know, the corpsman that looked like a boy became a man that day. He wasted no time moving through a hail of enemy bullets to reach the wounded Marine. The young corpsman tended to the injured Marine's wounds, then dragged him to a safer location. The Marine's wounds were so serious that we radioed in for an emergency medevac. A U.S. Army helicopter soon responded. That chopper came in with its machine guns blazing. It touched down for only a few moments, just long enough to get the wounded Marine and the young corpsman aboard.

Our understanding was that the wounded man had been shot through the neck and that the young corpsman had performed a lifesaving tracheotomy procedure on him. That young Navy corpsman never did return to our unit, nor did we ever know his name. We had referred to him only as "Doc." Sometime later, the word was passed that "Doc" had been awarded the Silver Star Medal with the Combat V (valor) for saving the life of that young Marine. Our thanks go out to all Navy corpsmen and Army medics who have served our country so valiantly throughout the years.

During one of our deployments into the mountains, we heard a story about a young Native American Marine from another platoon, whose name I never knew. He had earned quite a reputation for his courageous actions on the battlefields. And so the story of one of his encounters with the enemy was told to us. While walking point through a riverbed late one afternoon, he came face to face with an enemy soldier. Moments later, that NVA soldier lay dead in the shallow waters of the riverbed. We later learned that on the chest of that deceased NVA soldier was tattooed the phrase "Born in the North to Die in the South."

In September or October of 1968, we were again humping in the mountains when we happened to come upon a secluded swimming hole filled with cool mountain water. It wasn't the norm for us to let our guard down, but the stifling humidity of the day and the isolation of that location was too much of a temptation. We splashed around like a bunch of kids without a care in the world. Then it was time to move out again, back to the war.

When we were on major combat operations with one hundred to four hundred Marines, operations that could last for an extended period of time, we carried as much food, water, and combat gear as possible. We also carried several extra pairs of socks. Keeping our feet dry and powdered was of the utmost importance. When we were in the mountains, we would be re-supplied by helicopters whenever necessary depending, of course, on the weather conditions.

There was a constant turnover of names and faces as Marine combat casualties were removed from the battlefields. They were replaced by young Marines who were completely unaware of what the future held in store for them. No amount of training that they had received back in the states could have prepared them for what they were about to encounter, the horrors of man's inhumanity to man. During World War II, the average age of an American soldier was twenty-six. The average age of a combat Marine in Vietnam was nineteen to twenty years old.

Staff Sergeant D. J. Hinson Takes Over as Platoon Sergeant of the 3rd Platoon

On August 23, 1968, S/Sgt. D. J. Hinson took over as our platoon sergeant. He had enlisted in the Marine Corps in 1954 and would retire some twenty years later after having had a distinguished career in the Corps, a career that included two tours of duty in Vietnam, numerous combat medals, Vietnamese Gallantry Cross (for valor), Bronze Star Medal (for valor) and two Silver Star Medals (for valor), two Purple Hearts and other combat awards. He had been a drill instructor at Parris Island, South Carolina, in 1967 and 1968 and later would be a Marine Corps recruiter in Miami, Florida, in the early 1970s. S/Sgt. D.J. was a real Marine, a large man who was strong, intelligent, courageous, and a true leader. Before going out on combat missions, he would read to us from his personal Bible. He was responsible for saving the lives of many young Marines during our tour of duty in Vietnam. S/Sgt. D.J. was our leader, and we had the ultimate respect for him.

Early in November, 1968, we again went into the mountains. This time it was a battalion-size operation, four companies of Marines, a total of approximately four hundred men. I honestly don't remember much about what happened during the first month that we were out on that operation, but I do have some memories of what happened in December of 1968.

OPERATION SEARCH AND DESTROY

I wrote the next portion of this memoir in late December of 1968 when many of us were medevaced to the USS Sanctuary, *a Naval hospital ship stationed in the South China Sea just off the coast of South Vietnam, where we spent a period of time recovering from jungle rot, emersion foot, ringworm, and other combat related issues before returning to our unit.*

It was early December of 1968. The purpose of the operation was to search out and destroy known enemy elements taking refuge in the Dong Ha mountains of Vietnam. It was the seventh day of the operation, and thus far there had been only a few brief firefights with small groups of North Vietnamese soldiers.

The four companies of the Second Battalion 4th Marine Regiment had been sweeping on their own in certain designated areas within the mountains and were now closing in on the enemy's well-camouflaged and fortified positions. Fox Company was reportedly taking heavy small arms fire and Hotel Company was immediately dispatched to reinforce the Marines of Fox. The men of Golf Company were making their way through the treacherous mountain terrain in order to assist their fellow Marines in the combat that lay ahead.

As we made our way to the aid of our sister companies, the Marines of Golf 2/4 (better known as the Magnificent Bastards) could hear more and more clearly the sharp cracks of the enemy's automatic weapons fire. They could also distinguish the sounds of the Marines' M-60 machine guns and M-79 rounds exploding in that firefight.

As the day wore on, the physical strain on the advancing troopers of Golf Company became more and more apparent, but Captain Dwyer knew that this would vanish once his Marines made contact with the enemy. We were seasoned troops that had received constant training through the efforts of our staff and officers. The Marines of Golf Company had fought side by side during many previous battles, never giving up and following orders with no questions asked. The captain knew that these qualities were among the most important in the making of an outstanding infantry company.

It was late afternoon when G Company finally reached its objective, a ridgeline approximately 400 meters from the point of Fox and Hotel's firefight with the NVA. It was then we learned that both companies had sustained heavy casualties and had begun pulling back, carrying with them their dead and wounded, in order to set up a secure night defensive position. It wasn't long before the Phantom jets arrived and bombarded the area where the enemy was dug in. From our positions not far from the impact zone, it was plain to see the devastation brought upon the enemy force by our fearless brothers in the sky.

Then came the shower of artillery and naval gun fire which was to continue throughout the night in an attempt to limit the enemy's movements. At that time, when three of us were digging our foxhole in preparation for a possible enemy assault that could come during the course of the night, a single bullet from the rifle of an enemy sniper ended the life of yet another Marine. He had just recently returned to our unit after having spent a week with his young wife at a military R&R center in Hawaii. He was a good friend, a fine Marine, and would be missed by all.

Our field of fire was cleared and the trip flares and claymore mines were set out in front of our fighting holes. That night, each platoon was required to send out a four-man listening post approximately 40 meters in front of the perimeter. The sole purpose of this team was to act as an early warning system to detect any enemy movement and report such activity immediately over the radio.

A squad-size ambush was also sent out. That ambush was set up so that its field of fire could cover the enemy's most likely avenue of approach to the Marines' perimeter. Then came time for the Marines to rest but also to maintain a 50 percent security watch throughout the night. The hours of darkness passed slowly but without incident.

The next morning, at the first sign of daylight, S/Sgt. D.J. passed the word that at 0800 Golf Company would move through Fox and Hotel's positions and proceed until our point elements were engaged by the enemy. Then the commanders of Fox and Hotel Companies would maneuver their units to the enemy's flanks while Golf Company assaulted the NVA's fortifications.

It was approximately 0830 when G Company was moving through Fox and Hotel's locations with first squad, third platoon at the point. The Marines moved cautiously as they crept toward the enemy's bunker complex. First, they came upon several destroyed bamboo shelters. The area was thoroughly searched. A vast amount of enemy gear was found. Helmets, backpacks, blood-stained clothing, and Ho Chi Min sandals were scattered as far as the eye could see.

A four-man team was sent ahead to check out the area. We did not have far to go to find what we were looking for. We observed the area carefully. The entire area had been devastated by the previous day's bombardment. There were the charred remains of numerous enemy bunkers but no contact was made with the NVA. The enemy had obviously removed their dead and wounded from the battlefield. Swiftly and quietly, the point Marines made their way back and reported their observations to S/Sgt. D.J.

We had found the remains of a large enemy bunker complex and what had once been a vast ammunition storage area. The Phantom jets and the naval gunfire from the previous day's action had left a devastating impact on the area that no more than twenty-four hours ago had been thick jungle terrain. It was now barren of any living vegetation.

Fallen trees still smoldering from the previous day's action and the all-too-familiar odors of war left an unpleasant stench in the air. The Company was now moving in full strength toward the enemy bunker complex, fully aware of the consequences that would result if we were to be caught in the crossfire of an enemy ambush. As we moved upon the bunker complex, the tedious process of searching each individual bunker began. It wasn't until some time later when the search was nearing its end, that Captain Dwyer received a radio message from the lieutenant informing him that a prisoner had been captured.

Four men of the 3rd Platoon were retrieving gear that had been left behind by the enemy when a call came from a nearby bunker. "Hey, we got a live one in here." The four of us immediately dove for cover and focused our weapons on the bunker. The next thing we saw was S/Sgt. D.J. making his way over approximately 40 yards of open terrain and heading toward the enemy-occupied bunker. We all watched as he maneuvered his way to that bunker. Within moments, he leaped upon the enemy soldier and after a period of hand-to-hand combat, rendered the enemy incapable of further resistance. S/Sgt. D.J. had captured a prisoner of war.

The bunker was then searched for any additional enemy soldiers. There were none, but an AK-47 rifle and a .30-caliber machine gun were found along with hundreds of rounds of ammunition.

With those weapons at his disposal, that lone enemy soldier, had he not been captured by S/Sgt. D.J., might have caused the deaths of many Marines before he himself would have been killed.

During the interrogation of the prisoner, it was learned that the reinforced company of North Vietnamese soldiers, approximately three hundred men, had suffered heavy casualties during the battle with Fox and Hotel Companies and had moved during the night carrying with them their dead and wounded.

They were, in all probability, making their way back to the demilitarized zone (DMZ) where they could regroup and care for their wounded without fear of being attacked by the Marines in the neutral zone.

On December 11, 1968, one Golf Company Marine, three Hotel Company Marines, and eleven Fox Company Marines were killed in action in the mountains of Vietnam. The number of Marines that were wounded on that day is not known to me. May the people of our nation never forget the brave men and women who have given their lives throughout the history of our country for the freedoms we all enjoy.

After that operation was over, we landed on the helipad in Dong Ha, at which point S/Sgt. D.J. put us in formation and marched us into our base camp, calling cadence as we marched. I don't ever remember having been so proud to be one of my generation's sandlot soldiers, United States Marines. But we were also mindful of those Marines who were killed and wounded during that operation. (Semper Fi, S/Sgt. D.J.)

Without the helicopters, their pilots, and their crews, the casualty count of the American servicemen in Vietnam would have been many times higher than it was. The sound of the choppers coming in often replaced feelings of desperation with those of jubilation. Our thanks to them. They were heroes all, our fearless brothers in the sky!

As my memories are awakened on the hard times in troop movements and battles, other memories, lighter ones, of our lives cross my mind. When in the jungles and mountains of Vietnam, we ate two meals a day. Our food came in small cans called C-rations. There were twelve different meals available. My favorite was turkey loaf, peaches, and pound cake. Truly a meal fit for a king. Who could have asked for anything more?

While in the mountains, it was not uncommon for Sgt. D.J. to be roaming our hill with his hair clippers in hand. If you didn't want to get your head shaved, you better make yourself scarce. Really, Sgt. D.J., a high and tight while we were in the mountains? Bottom line was that if you were in S/Sgt D.J.'s platoon, you were going to look like a Marine whether you liked it or not.

Lance Corporal Ellis.
G 2/4. From Dallas, TX.
Vietnam

Lance Corporals Tami,
Bob and Lou, Golf 2/4.
Vietnam

"The rock pile."
Marine observation
base just off of
Route 9. I Corps.
South Vietnam, 1968

The Recon Mission
on the Ben Hai River

In late February of 1969, we had just returned to Dong Ha after some time in the mountains. We needed a rest. But then the word was passed that S/Sgt. D.J. was looking for a squad to go on a recon mission. Without thinking, we all grabbed our combat gear and reported to the command post. When we arrived, S/Sgt. D.J. was not there. We were told that a young lieutenant would be leading the mission. To say the least, we were not happy that S/Sgt. D.J. would not be leading us.

When we arrived at the chopper pad, there were four empty helicopters preparing to lift off. We boarded one of them and the pilots headed north. We were told that the choppers were en route to pick up a company of Marines inside the DMZ. When the choppers landed, we disembarked and took up a position in an old B-52 bomb crater.

There were thirteen of us, first squad 3rd Platoon, a machine-gun team, the lieutenant, a radio man, a dog handler, and a German shepherd. Not long after the four helicopters that were filled with nearly

100 combat Marines had left the area, we heard a number of enemy soldiers talking among themselves. Then one of them switched on a transistor radio and the music played well into the night. We were within a stone's throw from their location, yet they were completely unaware of our presence.

The plan was to spend the night in the bomb crater and attack the enemy just before sunrise. As planned, we crawled out of the bomb crater at dawn. We approached the unsuspecting enemy from a distance of approximately 40 yards. But in the excitement of the moment, one of our Marines advanced prematurely. Another nearly fatal breakdown of military discipline: we had lost the element of surprise.

When we reached the enemy's position, we came under AK-47 fire. The scout dog was hit by an AK round. Moments later, the dog's handler shot and killed the NVA soldier that fired that shot. The rest of the enemy fled, leaving behind all of their weapons, backpacks, and combat gear. I never did find out where that transistor radio ended up.

I have often wondered how many Marines would have lost their lives that morning on the banks of the Ben Hai River had it not been for the valiant actions of that scout dog and his handler, and yes, the dog did survive his wounds.

Within the captured NVA backpacks, we found maps, diagrams of different locations, and many pages of documents. We had radioed in for our team to be extracted by helicopter, and the choppers were on the way. We grabbed all that the enemy had left behind, including their rifles and a prized NVA flag.

I had many rules that I lived by while serving in Vietnam. Some of them were:

- Don't look at anything you don't need to look at.
- Don't lose your humanity.
- Focus on one day at a time.
- No souvenirs.
- No tunnels.

Whenever we came across enemy tunnels in the jungle, I was always amazed at the number of young Marines who would volunteer to take a flashlight and a .45-caliber pistol down into the enemy's underground tunnel systems. They were the bravest of the brave.

We returned to Dong Ha, and a day or so later, we were allowed to fly to the Marine base at Chu Lai in order to register our captured rifles as war trophies. When we arrived at the weapons registration office, we were told by the officer in charge that an NVA soldier could hit an ant in the ass from 1,000 meters with those sniper rifles.

REGISTRATION OF WAR TROPHY FIREARMS		
The original of this registration form will be retained by the person authorized possession. This registration is not transferrable.		
THIRD MARINE DIVISION IN THE FIELD VIETNAM Apr68-May69		
1. NAME OF OWNER (Last name, first name, middle initial) BURNS, William T.	3. SERVICE NUMBER 2418225	4. GRADE Cpl
5. ORGANIZATION "G" Co. 2d Bn. 4th Marines, 3d MarDiv	19 MAR 1969	
7. PERMANENT HOME ADDRESS (Street, city, state) 53 Ashley Rd, Holy Oke, Mass.	PROVOST MARSHAL OFFICE OFFICIAL CHHAC APO 96240	
DESCRIPTION OF FIREARM		
a. NAME SIMONOV	b. TYPE (Rifle, pistol, shotgun, SEMI-AUTOMATIC CARBINE	c. MODEL SKS
d. SERIAL NUMBER 171949	e. CALIBER 7.62mm	f. COUNTRY OF MANUFACTURE U.S.S.R.
8. DATE 6Mar69	9. TYPED NAME, GRADE, AND ORGANIZATION OF EXECUTING OFFICER B.K. JACKSON CAPT. G-2 COLLECTION OFFICER, 3D MARDIV	
10. STATION DONG HA COMBAT BASE, RVN	11. SIGNATURE OF EXECUTING OFFICER BKJackson	
DD FORM 603 OCT 51		PPC-Japan

When we returned to Dong Ha, we had no place to store our captured rifles. It was suggested that we leave them in a secure locker located in the company office. That sounded like a suitable solution. When the time came to retrieve our rifles, they were no longer there.

It was well known, at that time, that U.S. military personnel stationed on the island of Okinawa would pay up to $300 for a captured NVA rifle. While serving in Vietnam in 1969, a Marine Corporal was paid $255 a month "tax free." It always had been my intention to sell that captured rifle on our return to Okinawa.

Upon returning to our base camp, we took up our positions on the perimeter. We never did find out why S/Sgt. D.J. did not lead that recon patrol, but I do have my suspicions as to why he didn't. Bottom line is that every Marine that went out on that mission returned back to base safe and sound.

No matter where we were, whether it was the flatlands or in the mountains, we would always set up for the night on the highest hilltop in the area. That would ensure that if we were to be attacked by the enemy, we would have the advantage of the high ground. Every night we would send out an ambush team of approximately twelve to fifteen Marines (one squad and a four-man machine gun team). They would set up their ambush in the area that the enemy would most likely use to attack our perimeter.

In addition to the night ambush team, each platoon was required to send out a four-man LP (listening post) approximately forty yards in front of our fighting holes. Each team would carry a radio with them. Every thirty minutes the LP would be contacted by a Marine stationed in the captain's bunker. The message received by the LP would say "if all is secure, click your handset twice." That way the men on the listening post would not have to speak into the radio.

When the Marines were in combat, sleep was a luxury, not a necessity. I would estimate on a good night the average combat Marine would get approximately five hours of sleep. On those nights that we expected to be attacked by the enemy, the Marines would not sleep at all. It really is amazing how much the body can endure when it comes right down to life and death situations.

First squad 3rd platoon, Golf 2/4. Return to Marine Base. Dong Ha, Vietnam after recon mission.Ken, the author, Tami, O'Neil, McMann & Lt. Sawyer. February 1969

Operation Purple Martin

In early March of 1969, we were on another major combat operation. The name of it was Operation Purple Martin. It was a battalion-size operation, approximately four hundred Marines. There had been a lot of enemy activity in that area. A couple of Marine hilltop positions, not far from our location, had been overrun by the enemy in the early morning hours of February 25, 1969, resulting in the deaths of forty-three U.S. Marines and several Navy Corpsmen. There were more than one hundred Marines wounded during those battles on Fire Base Russell and Fire Base Neville. The NVA had also sustained heavy casualties during those attacks. At daybreak, the Marines found nearly seventy NVA bodies scattered about those hills.

On March 10, 1969, we were humping the ridgelines chasing ghosts again until the enemy decided they were in a position that gave them the tactical advantage. We were point squad that day, and our point man was the first to get hit. As the firefight intensified, I was struck by an AK-47 round that caused considerable damage to my left hand. Soon after that, one of our machine gun teams sprayed the area where the enemy had positioned themselves with two hundred rounds of 7.62. The battle then subsided temporarily. The wounded were taken back to the hilltop where we had spent the previous night.

Another company of Marines had taken over the hill. They were digging foxholes and putting out trip flares and claymore mines in preparation for an enemy assault. As part of their defense of the hill, that company had sent out four 4-man observation teams approximately 40 yards below the hilltop, one team north, one east, one south, and one west. About an hour after we reached the hill, a firefight broke out on the east side of the hill.

The Marines radioed in that they had killed four enemy soldiers who were attempting to breech the hilltop. Approximately ten minutes later, the exact same scenario took place on the west side of the hill with the exact same results. Another radio message came in. They had killed four NVA soldiers who were attempting to penetrate our perimeter.

It should be noted that for the enemy to attack a fortified Marine position in broad daylight meant that we were surrounded by a large force of enemy soldiers. Early that evening, a medevac chopper and several helicopter gunships came in under enemy fire and removed all of the wounded from the hilltop. The fighting continued throughout the night and for many days and nights that followed.

The War Was Over for the Wounded

We were flown to a field hospital in Quang Tri where the doctors performed the initial medical procedures on all of the wounded. A day or so later, we were flown to an American Military Hospital in Japan. We spent several days there before continuing on to a U.S. Military Hospital on the island of Guam, where we spent several weeks before returning to the United States.

I saw a lot of other wounded Marines while on the island of Guam. We had the opportunity to spend some time with S/Sgt. D.J. He had been wounded once on March 10 and then again on March 11, 1968. We were all happy to see that he had survived the battle.

The fighting was over for the wounded. We were transported back to the U.S. and treated for our injuries at military hospitals nearest to our hometowns. I spent a period of time at a Naval hospital just outside of Boston. While there, many of us received citations and combat metals.

I was promoted to Sergeant E-5 on September 1, 1969.

The war continued until 1975. To this day, the memories of those Marines who lost their lives on the battlefields are still fresh in my mind.

I have, over these many years, often wondered how it was possible for so many sandlot soldiers to have survived their experiences in Vietnam. The only explanation I can come up with is that we must have had angels riding on our shoulders. During the years of the war, 2.7 million Americans served in Vietnam. More than fifty-eight thousand courageous young patriots were killed in action. More than three hundred thousand U.S. military personnel were wounded, many of whom returned home with physical challenges and the difficulties of coping with the memories of the war.

Challenges that were not unlike those faced by all of the brave men and women who have fought our country's battles throughout the history of our nation.

I was medically retired from the United States Marine Corps on February 20, 1970, a twenty-year-old Sergeant E-5.

It was never my intention in the writing of this memoir to glorify the actions of man's inhumanity to man. Recounting my own experience is meant to be a lesson, a history lesson that if not learned is destined to be the future of mankind.

The M-16 Rifle

No memories of the Vietnam War would be complete without a conversation pertaining to the M-16 rifle. A lot has been written over the past fifty years with regard to the pros and cons of the main battle rifle used by the American soldier during the Vietnam War. But one simple fact is undisputable: The enemy's AK-47 rifle was designed to accommodate a 30-round magazine, whereas the M-16 rifle was designed to accommodate only a 20-round magazine. Therefore, during a five-magazine firefight, the enemy's AK-47 rifle would fire 150 rounds while the American soldier's M-16 rifle, with the same number of magazines, would fire a maximum of only 100 rounds. (End of conversation)

A Marine's Marine

Finding Gy/S/Sgt. D.J. Forty-Eight Years After Vietnam

In 2017, my wife, Stella, located Gy/S/Sgt. D.J. We had not seen each other for nearly fifty years. It was great to talk with him and reminisce about some of the times we had spent together while in Vietnam. At that point, we sent Gy/S/Sgt. D.J. a copy of my 1968 writing "Operation Search and Destroy." Several days later, Gy/S/Sgt. D.J. replied via email:

Hi Bill and Stella,

Yes, I remember that night very well and remember often repeating the 23rd Psalm from the Bible which reads in part, "Yea, though I walk through the valley of the shadow of death, I will fear no evil; thy rod and thy staff, they comfort me." I knew we were going into a "valley of death" and I could sense much fear and foreboding, not only in myself but in our troops. Needless to say, that Psalm was a great comfort. And what happened the next day? The enemy had fled.

Now I will tell you "THE REST OF THE STORY," as Paul Harvey used to say. At the time we captured that NVA soldier, there was going on, in Paris, France, "peace talks" and one of the objectives of the Americans was to show that the NVA were not living up to the peace agreement they had signed, which stated they would not go beyond the neutral zone that had been established. Our negotiating team was trying to prove the NVA were lying. So, the day we captured that NVA where they were not supposed to be, our battalion commander flew out, picked him up and within three days, that little NVA soldier was sitting in a room where the Paris peace talks were taking place. The NVA were caught in their own lies and our team had living proof they were lying. End of the story.

More of what happened after that: The same battalion commander put me in for a battle field commission.

Regards,
S/Sgt. D.J.

Donald J. Hinson was and always will be a Marine's Marine. I want to share a bit of his exemplary military history because he was such a strong influence on the men he led.

Donald was born on October 7, 1936, in St. Augustine, FL, one of 11 children. In September of 1942, Donald's oldest brother, Howard Brice Hinson, enlisted in the United States Marine Corps. During the years of World War II, he fought in the battles of the Marshall Islands, Saipan, and Tinian before being killed in action on February 14, 1945, during the Marine's battle against the Japanese Army on the island of Iwo Jima.

On March 13, 1954, at age 17, Donald, following in the footsteps of his older brother, enlisted in the United States Marine Corps. On May 17, 1958, Lance Corporal Hinson and Mary Louise

Hummel were married in Miami, FL. Many have said that the wives of our military men are now, and have been throughout our history, the unsung heroes of our nation. Gunny Hinson and Mary Lou, who has passed away, were married for nearly 60 years and had three children.

PROMOTIONS

Donald was promoted to PFC April 10, 1954, to Marine corporal April 18, 1960, and to sergeant December 1, 1963. In August of 1965, he participated in the first major battle of the Vietnam war, Operation Starlight. On August 1, 1966, he was promoted to Staff Sergeant.

On May 15, 1966, after completing his first tour of duty in Vietnam, Sergeant Hinson returned to the U.S. and was assigned to Parris Island, SC, where he spent the next two years as a Drill Instructor. August 23, 1965, he was assigned to duty as infantry unit leader in Company G, 2nd Battalion 4th Marines, 3rd Marine Division, Vietnam.

MEDALS, AWARDS, AND CITATIONS AWARDED GY/SGT. HINSON DURING HIS 20-YEAR CAREER

- Two Silver Star Medals (V)
- Two Bronze Stars (V)
- Two Purple Hearts
- Combat Action Ribbon
- Presidential Unit Citation

- Meritorious Unit Commendation

- Good Conduct Medal

- National Defense Medal

- Vietnamese Cross of Gallantry with Bronze Star on November 1968 for outstanding combat actions on 20 October 1968

Bronze Star Medal (V) for heroic achievement in combat December 12, 1968. Text of the award citation follows.

> *For heroic achievement in connection with operations against the enemy in the Republic of Vietnam while serving Company G, 2nd Battalion, 4th Marines, 3rd Marine Division. On 12 December 1968, while conducting search and destroy operations near Dong Ha Mountain in Quang Tri Province, Staff/Sgt. Hinson's platoon located a hostile bunker complex, and as the Marines were searching the emplacements, a North Vietnamese soldier was found hiding in a fortification. Rapidly assessing the situation, Staff/Sgt. Hinson unhesitatingly elected to enter the position and attempt to capture the enemy. Disregarding his own safety, he fearlessly moved inside the bunker and, disarming the hostile soldier, led him out of his hiding place. His bold initiative and resolute determination inspired all who observed him and were instrumental in capturing the North Vietnamese soldier and various items of equipment and ordnance. Staff/Sgt. Hinson's courage, aggressive leadership and steadfast devotion to duty in the face of great personal danger were in keeping with the highest traditions of the Marine Corps and the U.S. Naval Service.*

Silver Star Medal (V) for conspicuous gallantry and intrepidity in action on March 11, 1969. Text of award citation follows:

For conspicuous gallantry and intrepidity in action while serving as a platoon commander with Company G, 2nd Battalion, Fourth Marines, Third Marine Division in connection with combat operations against the enemy in the Republic of Vietnam. On the afternoon of 11 March, 1969, during operation Purple Martin, Company G was moving towards its objective Hill 477, two miles northeast of Fire Support Base Neville, when the Marines came under intense automatic weapons fire from the numerically superior North Vietnamese Army Force. When the forward elements became pinned down and had sustained several casualties, Staff/Sgt. Hinson was directed to move forward with a reserve force to assist the Marines that were in contact with the enemy. Responding immediately, he quickly moved his platoon to the area of the firefight, and then repeatedly exposed himself to hostile fire as he moved from one position to another, directing the fire of his men and shouting words of encouragement. When he was informed that a Marine casualty was lying in a dangerously exposed area forward of the friendly lines, Staff/Sgt. Hinson fearlessly maneuvered across the fire-swept terrain, throwing grenades as he advanced, and with the aid of another Marine was successful in retrieving the casualty. After returning to his platoon's position, he sustained a serious wound, but steadfastly refused medical treatment and assisted the other casualties. Only after all of his men had returned to friendly lines and all the other evacuees were aboard medical evacuation helicopters, did Staff/Sgt. Hinson agree to be evacuated. His heroic and timely actions inspired all who observed him and were instrumental in defeating the enemy force. By his courage, aggressive leadership, and unwavering devotion to duty in the face of great personal danger, Staff/Sgt. Hinson upheld the highest traditions of the Marine Corps and of the United States Naval Service.

WORDS FROM COMMANDING OFFICERS

Statement of Major John E. Seeburger, Jr., USMC

During the period 10 October 1965 to 18 February 1966 while serving as Commanding Officer of Company L, 3rd Battalion, 4th Marines, I was fortunate enough to have Staff/Sgt. (then sgt.) Donald Hinson as a member of my command. Sgt. Hinson served as a squad leader and occasionally as right guide in the 3rd Platoon of Company L. During this time, Sgt. Hinson's performance was one of an extremely high caliber. Sgt. Hinson was an extremely competent and conscientious Marine of unquestionable courage and fortitude. His military presence, bearing and manner were always impeccable. He was particularly thoughtful of his subordinates and commanded their respect because they knew he was looking out for them. He was very religious and inspirational to his comrades. In this respect, a remarkable efficient and capable moral example to all. Sgt. Hinson was a "no-nonsense" leader who accomplished every mission by the most positive traits of leadership. He was a most loyal NCO and to this day I consider it a privilege to have commanded a Marine NCO such as Sgt. Hinson. He personified the traits associated with outstanding combat leadership. It is noteworthy that during this period of time in a combat environment, almost the entire time under the most adverse weather conditions, usually with an under strength unit and under the constant strain of a squad leader in contact with or searching for the enemy, Sgt. Hinson's morale remained unusually high as did that of his men, a tribute to his leadership.

— *Major John E, Seeburger, Jr., USMC*

On June 25, 1968, Meritorious Mast. Letter from commanding officer, G. C. Koontz, Second Recruit Training Battalion, Parris Island, SC to Staff Sergeant D.J. Hinson

While serving as a member of this command during the period July 1966 to June 1968; in the capacity as assistant drill instructor, senior drill instructor and battalion career advisory NCO you have demonstrated the highest degree of military bearing and professional competence during the period August 1966 to January 1968. You worked one recruit platoon as an assistant drill instructor and five recruit platoons as a senior drill instructor in a diligent, competent and professional manner constantly displaying a zealous devotion to duty. You eagerly accepted the responsibility by your own initiative and dedication to spend many off duty hours working with the more slow learner and physically weak recruits thus insuring that they developed into soundly trained basic Marines. During your time as a senior drill instructor, you were directly responsible for training over four hundred recruits. Your dedication and devotion to duty throughout has earned for you the respect and admiration of contemporaries and seniors alike and may I add, my personal congratulations on a job well done.

— *Commanding Officer G. C. Koontz*

His Commanding Officer in Company G, Captain Joseph M. Dwyer, considered Staff/Sgt. Hinson to be the finest Staff/Sergeant he has served with and prepared a recommendation for a combat leadership commission for Staff/Sgt. Hinson in April 1969.

Staff/Sgt. Hinson exemplifies the word leadership in his every action. Of him it can truly be said, he is the leader of men. During his tour, he served as Platoon Sergeant and Platoon Commander. During the many contacts with the enemy he was acting as Platoon Commander. His leadership and courage, and his decisiveness and coolness under fire were well beyond of that normally expected of Staff NCO's and was equal to and sometimes above, the level of what would be considered an excellent Officer Platoon Commander. This was reflected in the incident when Staff/Sgt. Hinson led his platoon in the attack. Staff/Sgt. Hinson was very seriously wounded yet he refused to be medevac'd."

— *Captain Joseph M. Dwyer*

Additional words from Captain Joseph M. Dwyer

"It is with a high degree of respect and enthusiasm that I recommend Staff/Sgt. Hinson for a battlefield commission. This recommendation emanates not solely from the reward deserved Staff/Sgt. Hinson, but from the sincere belief that Staff/Sgt. Hinson's potential can be realized only by his assuming the increased responsibility inherent in the officer ranks.

— *Captain Joseph M. Dwyer*

Words from Reporting Senior Officer Joseph E. Hopkins, Lt. Col., USMC

Staff/Sgt. Hinson displays personal and moral values of the very highest quality. He is positively a Marine of officer quality, with outstanding potential to develop and serve with maximum efficiency in an officer billet and role. I consider him to be one of the finest Marines I have ever known and he absolutely is in the very highest bracket ever among superior staff NCO's.

— *Reporting Senior Officer: Joseph E. Hopkins, Lt. Col., USMC*

Gy/Sgt. Hinson retired from the United States Marine Corps on July 24, 1974, after 20 years of distinguished service to our nation.

G/Sgt. Donald J. Hinson (far right), Platoon Sergent, 3rd Platoon Golf 2/4, with numerous Golf 2/4 Marines, March 1969. Photo taken only days prior to the start of Operation Purple Martin.

GY/SGT. HINSON WITH FAMILY AND FRIEND

me as an escort for miss USA-1970

GY/SGT. D.J. HINSON ESCORTING MISS USA 1970

S/SGT. DONALD J. HINSON
SENIOR DRILL INSTRUCTION PLATOON 295
PARRIS ISLAND, SC.
GRADUATION DATE: AUGUST 28, 1967

GY/SGT. D.J. HINSON WITH WIFE MARY LOUISE, 2017

Gy/Sgt. Donald J. Hinson

Was our platoon leader while serving in Vietnam

in 1968 - 1969

He was our leader and every Marine in our

entire battalion had the ultimate respect for him

Semper Fi, Gy/Sgt. D.J.

Marine Gy/Sgt. Donald J. Hinson

is a retired United States Marine

whose military career began in 1954.

Over the next twenty years Gy/Sgt. D.J. repeatedly

distinguished himself on and off the battlefield.

Those of us who were privileged to have served with him

during the Vietnam War were witness to his

unwavering dedication to his Marines and to the Corps.

The gallantry that Gy/Sgt. D.J. displayed on so many occasions

during that war inspired many young Marines.

The men of the 3rd Platoon, Golf Company

2nd Battalion 4th Marine Regiment

salute you, Gy/Sgt. D.J.,

for you truly are a Marine's Marine.

Semper Fi

The Incident
at the
New River Bridge

In the year 1957, then a young Corporal, Donald J. Hinson,

was a member of the Jacksonville, North Carolina

Military Police Department.

While on a routine night patrol accompanied by

three other Marine MP's, they witnessed a horrific

accident involving two vehicles on the New River Bridge.

Despite the fact that both vehicles were engulfed in flames,

and with complete disregard for their own safety,

the Marines, led by Corporal Hinson, rushed to the vehicles,

extracted the injured, and carried them to a safe location.

Due to the heroic actions of the Marines, three of the four

occupants of the vehicles survived the accident.

Semper Fi, Sgt. D.J.

THE AUTHOR, CPL. W. THOMAS BURNS, GOLF 2/4
ELEPHANT GRASS—
LIKE WALKING THROUGH RAZOR BLADES
VIETNAM, 1968

CITATIONS & AWARDS

SGT. W. THOMAS BURNS

VIETNAM

1968 & 1969

To all who shall see these presents, greeting:

Know Ye, that reposing special trust and confidence in the fidelity and abilities of William J. Burns 2418225 / 0331 *, I do appoint* him a Sergeant *in the*

United States Marine Corps

to rank as such from the first *day of* September *, nineteen hundred and* sixty nine.

This appointee will therefore carefully and diligently discharge the duties of the grade to which appointed by doing and performing all manner of things thereunto pertaining. And I do strictly charge and require all personnel of lesser grade to render obedience to appropriate orders. And this appointee is to observe and follow such orders and directions as may be given from time to time by Superiors acting according to the rules and articles governing the discipline of the Armed Forces of the United States of America

Given under my hand at Marine Barracks, U. S. Naval Base, Boston, Mass. *this* eighth *day of* September *, in the year of our Lord nineteen hundred and* sixty nine.

AUTHORITY MCBul 1430 of 6 September 1969
and par 3025.1c(1) MARCORPROMMAN
DATE OF PROMOTION 8 September 1969
This appointment is effective for all
purposes, including pay and allowances
on 8 September 1969 (PURSUANT PROV
MCBUL 1430 of 6 September 1969)

E. H. MACKEL, Col. USMC
Commanding

DD FORM
1 SEP 54 216MC
S/N 0102-002-0800

To all who shall see these presents, greeting:

Know Ye, that reposing special trust and confidence in the fidelity and abilities

of   William T. Burns 2418225/0331   , I do

appoint him a   Corporal   *in the*

United States Marine Corps

to rank as such from the   first   *day of*   January   , *nineteen*

hundred and sixty nine

This appointee will therefore carefully and diligently discharge the duties of the grade to which appointed by doing and performing all manner of things thereunto pertaining. And I do strictly charge and require all personnel of lesser grade to render obedience to appropriate orders. And this appointee is to observe and follow such orders and directions as may be given from time to time by Superiors acting according to the rules and articles governing the discipline of the

Armed Forces of the United States of America

Given under my hand at   Headquarters, 2d Battalion, 4th Marines
3d Marine Division (Rein) FMF, FPO SFRAN 96602

this   fifteenth   *day of* January   , *in the year of our Lord nineteen*

hundred and sixty nine

AUTHORITY MCBul 1418 of 14Mar68

DATE OF PROMOTION 15 January 1969

J. E. HOPKINS, LtCol, USMC
Commanding B

DD FORM 278MC
1 SEP 54

THE UNITED STATES OF AMERICA

THIS IS TO CERTIFY THAT
THE PRESIDENT OF THE UNITED STATES OF AMERICA
HAS AWARDED THE

BRONZE STAR MEDAL

(WITH COMBAT "V")

TO

CORPORAL WILLIAM T. BURNS, UNITED STATES MARINE CORPS

FOR

HEROIC ACHIEVEMENT ON 10 MARCH 1969

S   25TH   DAY OF   JULY   1969

SECRETARY OF THE NAVY

The President of the United States takes pleasure in presenting the BRONZE STAR MEDAL to

CORPORAL WILLIAM T. BURNS

UNITED STATES MARINE CORPS

for service as set forth in the following

CITATION:

"For heroic achievement in connection with combat operations against the enemy in the Republic of Vietnam while serving as a Squad Leader with Company G, Second Battalion, Fourth Marines, Third Marine Division. On the morning of 10 March 1969, during Operation Purple Martin, the Third Platoon of Company G was engaged in assaulting a numerically superior enemy force near Hill 477 in the northern I Corps Tactical Zone. When his unit came under a heavy volume of hostile automatic weapons and grenade fire, Corporal Burns, with complete disregard for his own safety, moved across more than forty-five meters of fire-swept terrain as he quickly organized his squad. Despite receiving a serious fragmentation wound in his left hand, he resolutely continued to lead his men, skillfully directing their fire upon the enemy emplacements and offering them words of encouragement. Administering emergency first aid to the more seriously wounded Marines, he refused to accept medical attention until all other casualties had been treated. His bold initiative and sincere concern for the welfare of his comrades inspired all who observed him and were instrumental in defeating the hostile force. Corporal Burns' courage, aggressive fighting spirit and steadfast devotion to duty in the face of great personal danger contributed significantly to the accomplishment of his unit's mission and were in keeping with the highest traditions of the Marine Corps and of the United States Naval Service."

The Combat Distinguishing Device is authorized.

FOR THE PRESIDENT,

H. W. BUSE, JR.
LIEUTENANT GENERAL, U. S. MARINE CORPS
COMMANDING GENERAL, FLEET MARINE FORCE, PACIFIC

DEPARTMENT OF THE NAVY

THIS IS TO CERTIFY THAT
THE SECRETARY OF THE NAVY HAS AWARDED THE

NAVY ACHIEVEMENT MEDAL

(WITH COMBAT "V")

TO

CORPORAL WILLIAM T. BURNS, UNITED STATES MARINE CORPS

FOR

MERITORIOUS SERVICE FROM 2 MAY 1968 TO 1 MARCH 1969

GIVEN THIS   14TH DAY OF   APRIL 19 69

SECRETARY OF THE NAVY

The Secretary of the Navy takes pleasure in presenting the NAVY ACHIEVEMENT MEDAL to

CORPORAL WILLIAM THOMAS BURNS

UNITED STATES MARINE CORPS

for outstanding achievement in the superior performance of his duties in the field of leadership achievement as set forth in the following

CITATION:

"While serving as a Fire Team Leader with Company G, Second Battalion, Fourth Marines, Third Marine Division in connection with operations against the enemy in the Republic of Vietnam from 2 May 1968 to 1 March 1969, Corporal Burns performed his duties in an exemplary manner. Participating in five major combat operations, including Operations Napoleon/Saline and Scotland II, he repeatedly distinguished himself by his courage and composure under fire. In July 1968, a large enemy force launched an aggressive assault on the Company G defensive position at Hill 606. Alertly observing several wounded Marines pinned down in an area dangerously exposed to hostile fire, Corporal Burns immediately deployed his men to provide effective fire which enabled the injured men to move to more covered positions. Constantly concerned for the combat readiness of his unit, he tirelessly trained his men and molded them into an effective fighting force. Corporal Burns' leadership, professional competence and steadfast devotion to duty reflect great credit upon himself, the Marine Corps and the Naval Service."

Corporal Burns is authorized to wear the Combat "V".

FOR THE SECRETARY OF THE NAVY,

H. W. BUSE, JR.
LIEUTENANT GENERAL, U. S. MARINE CORPS
COMMANDING GENERAL, FLEET MARINE FORCE, PACIFIC

THE UNITED STATES OF AMERICA

TO ALL WHO SHALL SEE THESE PRESENTS, GREETING:
THIS IS TO CERTIFY THAT
THE PRESIDENT OF THE UNITED STATES OF AMERICA
HAS AWARDED THE

PURPLE HEART

ESTABLISHED BY GENERAL GEORGE WASHINGTON
AT NEWBURGH, NEW YORK, AUGUST 7, 1782
TO

CORPORAL WILLIAM T. BURNS, UNITED STATES MARINE CORPS

FOR WOUNDS RECEIVED IN ACTION
REPUBLIC OF VIETNAM, 10 MARCH 1969
GIVEN UNDER MY HAND IN THE CITY OF WASHINGTON
THIS 17TH   DAY OF APRIL   19 69

GENERAL, U.S. MARINE CORPS
COMMANDANT OF THE MARINE CORPS

NAVMC HO 555 (REV. 5-62) (1650)

TRANSMITTAL OF AND/OR ENTITLEMENT TO AWARDS

WILLIAMS T BURNS	MARINE CORPS 17 Apr 96 REG

A review of your record indicates that you are eligible for the following awards. The following authorized awards are enclosed.

BRONZE STAR MEDAL - With Combat "v".
COMBAT ACTION RIBBON - No citation shown.
NATIONAL DEFENSE SERVICE MEDAL
NAVY ACHIEVEMENT MEDAL - With Combat "v"
NAVY UNIT COMMENDATION RIBBON - Citation.
PURPLE HEART MEDAL
VIETNAM SERVICE MEDAL - With four bronze stars
MARINE CORPS MARKSMAN RIFLE BADGE
REPUBLIC OF VIETNAM CAMPAIGN MEDAL -FOREIGN
REP VIETNAM MUC GALLANTRY CROSS-FOREIGN
REP VIETNAM MUC CIVIL ACTIONS MEDAL- FOREIGN

COMMENTS: All available citations and certificate are enclosed. Navy Achievement, Bronze Star, Navy Unit, and the Purple Heart. See attached Document.

Foreign awards, stars, badges and insignias are not stocked or issued by the Navy Department but may be obtained from civilian dealers of military supply stores.

WILLIAMS BURNS	12 BUREAU OF NAVAL PERSONNEL RETIRED RECORDS SECTION (PERS-313B) 9700 PAGE AVENUE ST. LOUIS, MO 63132

1781/1781 -8-9-26-30-38-41-44-63-78-79-80

NAVPERS 1650/65 (7-91)

18

THE SECRETARY OF THE NAVY

WASHINGTON

The Secretary of the Navy takes pleasure in presenting the NAVY UNIT COMMENDATION to

BATTALION LANDING TEAM
SECOND BATTALION, FOURTH MARINES

for service as set forth in the following

CITATION:

For outstanding heroism in action against insurgent communist forces in the northern I Corps Area, Republic of Vietnam, from 5 March to 31 May 1968. Assigned the mission of keeping the vital Cua Viet River open from Dong Ha to the coast, the Battalion Landing Team was helilifted on 5 March to the vicinity of Mai Xa Canh, a village in the coastal area east of Dong Ha. An operation was immediately launched to seek out and destroy certain North Vietnamese Army forces which had been interrupting the flow of logistics traffic on the Cua Viet. Aggressive patrolling and extensive sweeps resulted in numerous engagements with the enemy and a decrease in his overactivity. The Battalion Landing Team's Area of Responsibility in the Mai Xa Canh vicinity was the operating and infiltration route for six enemy units. Avoiding a direct confrontation with the Marines, the infiltrators skirted the Battalion Landing Team's Area of Responsibility and established themselves to the west at the village of Dai Do. Learning of the enemy's plan, the Team advanced on Dai Do on 30 April and was met by a well equipped adversary, firmly entrenched in heavily fortified bunkers, supported by heavy artillery, and determined to fight to the last. In the three days of savage fighting that ensued, the stubborn enemy was slowly and painfully driven from his defense positions. During the Battalion Landing Team's three-month stay in the Cua Viet area, the river remained open, having been closed only during the battle for Dai Do. The Battalion Landing Team successfully accomplished its assigned mission while inflicting devastating losses on the enemy in terms of men killed and equipment lost. By their effective teamwork, aggressive fighting spirit, and individual acts of heroism and daring, the men of the Battalion Landing Team and supporting aviation units not only achieved significant results, but in doing so exemplified qualities of courage and skill which were in keeping with the highest traditions of the Marine Corps and the United States Naval Service.

WASHINGTON ADDRESS:
239 CANNON HOUSE OFFICE BUILDING
WASHINGTON, D.C. 20515
AREA CODE 202
PHONE: 225-5335

DISTRICT OFFICE:
7 NORTH STREET
PITTSFIELD, MASS. 01201
AREA CODE 413
PHONE: 442-0946

Congress of the United States
House of Representatives
Washington, D. C.

TREASURY AND POST OFFICE
FOREIGN OPERATIONS
TRANSPORTATION

SELECT COMMITTEE ON
SMALL BUSINESS
SUBCOMMITTEES:
GOVERNMENT PROCUREMENT
REGULATORY AGENCIES
TAXATION

MIGRATORY BIRD
CONSERVATION COMMISSION

JOINT COMMISSION
ON THE COINAGE

March 20, 1969

Mr. William J. Burns
53 Ashley Road
Holyoke, Massachusetts 01040

Dear Mr. Burns:

I regret very much to learn of the injury to your son, Corporal William T. Burns, U. S. Marine, in Vietnam.

My Pittsfield Office advised me that you had received only one report from the Marine Corps on his injury and were anxious to know his present condition, and whether he would be returned to a hospital in the United States.

I took this up with the U. S. Marine Corps here and they reported that your son was in the U. S. Naval Hospital in Guam, and that his condition is good and his prognosis is good.

His address there, if you wish to write to him, is:

U.S. Naval Hospital
Guam
c/o FPO San Francisco 96630.

The Marine Corps has requested a report from the Medical Authorities at the hospital as to when your son might return to the United States, if they plan to return him here for treatment.

As soon as I receive further word, I shall be glad to advise you.

With my best wishes to you and your son, I am

Cordially yours,

Silvio O. Conte
Member of Congress

SOC:C

PHYSICAL EVALUATION BOARD, FIRST NAVAL DISTRICT
Naval Hospital
Chelsea, Massachusetts 02150

ND1/361/5420
13 January 1970

From: Physical Evaluation Board
To: Sgt. William Thomas Burns, USMC, 2418225
Marine Barracks, Charlestown, Massachusetts 02129
Via: Designated Counsel for the Party LTJG L.R. Small, USNR

Subj: Prima facie recommended findings of a Physical Evaluation Board

1. A Physical Evaluation Board met on 13 January 1970 to consider your case; and solely on the basis of a review of the records, the board intends to recommend approval of the following prima facie findings:

   a. It is recommended that Sgt. William Thomas Burns, USMC, 2418225 be found

(1) Unfit to perform the duties of his grade because of physical disability

   1. GUNSHOT WOUND, LEFT HAND, #8830-4411
   2. TRAUMATIC AMPUTATION, LEFT MIDDLE FINGER, #8870-410
   3. COMPOUND FRACTURE, 2ND AND 3RD METACARPALS, LEFT, #8150-442
   4. ABSENCE OF PROXIMAL ONE-HALF OF MID PHALANX AND DISTAL TIP OF PROXIMAL PHALANX, 4TH FINGER, LEFT, #8160-444
   5. ABNORMAL SENSATION, ULNAR BORDER, 2ND FINGER AND 3CM AREA WITH ABNORMAL SENSATION AT BASE F 2ND FINGER, LEFT HAND PALMER ASPECT, #3680-474
   6. LIMITATION OF MOTION OF WRIST, #8829

(2) That such disability was incurred while entitled to receive basic pay.

(3) That such disability is not due to intentional misconduct or willful neglect and was not incurred during a period of unauthorized absence.

(4) (b) That such disability was incurred in line of duty in time of National Emergency.

(5) That such disability is rated at 60% In accordance with the standard Schedule for Rating Disabilities in current use by the Veterans' Administration.

   5131   50%
   5215   10%

(6) That accepted medical principles indicate that such disability is permanent.

CERTIFICATE OF RETIREMENT
FROM THE ARMED FORCES OF THE UNITED STATES OF AMERICA

TO ALL WHO SHALL SEE THESE PRESENTS, GREETING:
THIS IS TO CERTIFY THAT

SERGEANT WILLIAM THOMAS BURNS 241 82 25

HAVING SERVED FAITHFULLY AND HONORABLY
WAS RETIRED FROM THE

UNITED STATES MARINE CORPS

ON THE   TWENTIETH   DAY OF   FEBRUARY
ONE THOUSAND NINE HUNDRED AND   SEVENTY

WASHINGTON, D. C.

GENERAL, UNITED STATES MARINE CORPS
COMMANDANT OF THE MARINE CORPS

DD FORM 363-MC 1 AUG 63 (1189)

About the Author

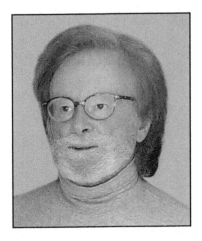

W. Thomas Burns is an avid sports enthusiast who, at the tender age of ten, began caddying at the local golf course and thus began his life-long passion for the game of golf. After graduating from high school in 1967, he enlisted in the United States Marine Corps where after four months of training, he spent the nineteenth year of his life in the mountains and jungles of Vietnam. In 1970 he was medically retired from the Marine Corps, a twenty-year-old sergeant E-5. The author is now retired and living with his wife, Stella ("Star"), in the beautiful state of North Carolina. He is also the author of *The Magical Christmas Tree Room, A Holiday Tale.*

Made in the USA
Las Vegas, NV
16 March 2022

45794736R00056